How to use this book

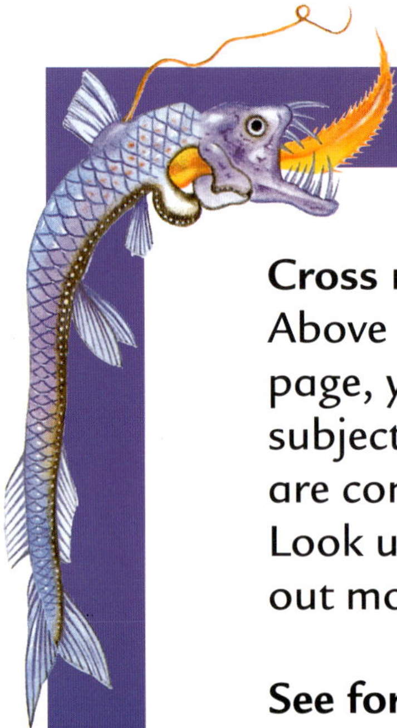

Cross references
Above the heading on the page, you will find a list of subjects in the book which are connected to the topic. Look up these pages to find out more about the subjects.

See for yourself
See for yourself bubbles give you the chance to test out some of the ideas in this book. They explain what you will need and what you have to do to see if an idea really works.

Quiz corner
In the quiz corner, you will find a list of questions. The answers to the quiz questions are somewhere on the two pages. Can you answer all the questions about each topic?

Glossary
Difficult words are explained in the glossary near the back of the book. These words are in **bold** on the page. Look them up in the glossary to find out what they mean.

Index
The index is at the back of the book. It is a list of words about everything mentioned in the book, with page numbers next to the words. The list is in the same order as the alphabet. If you want to find out about a subject, look up the word in the index, then turn to the page number given.

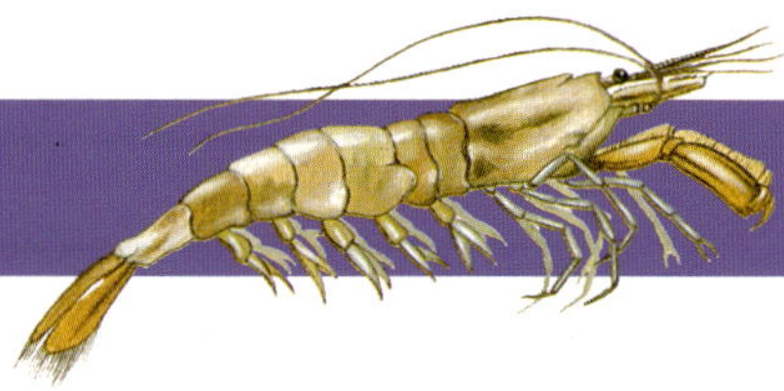

Contents

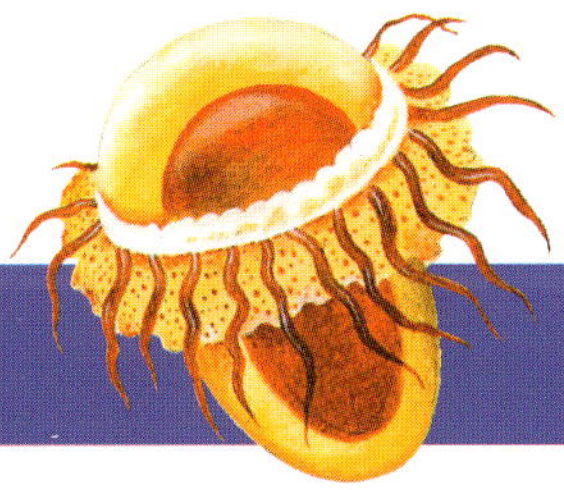

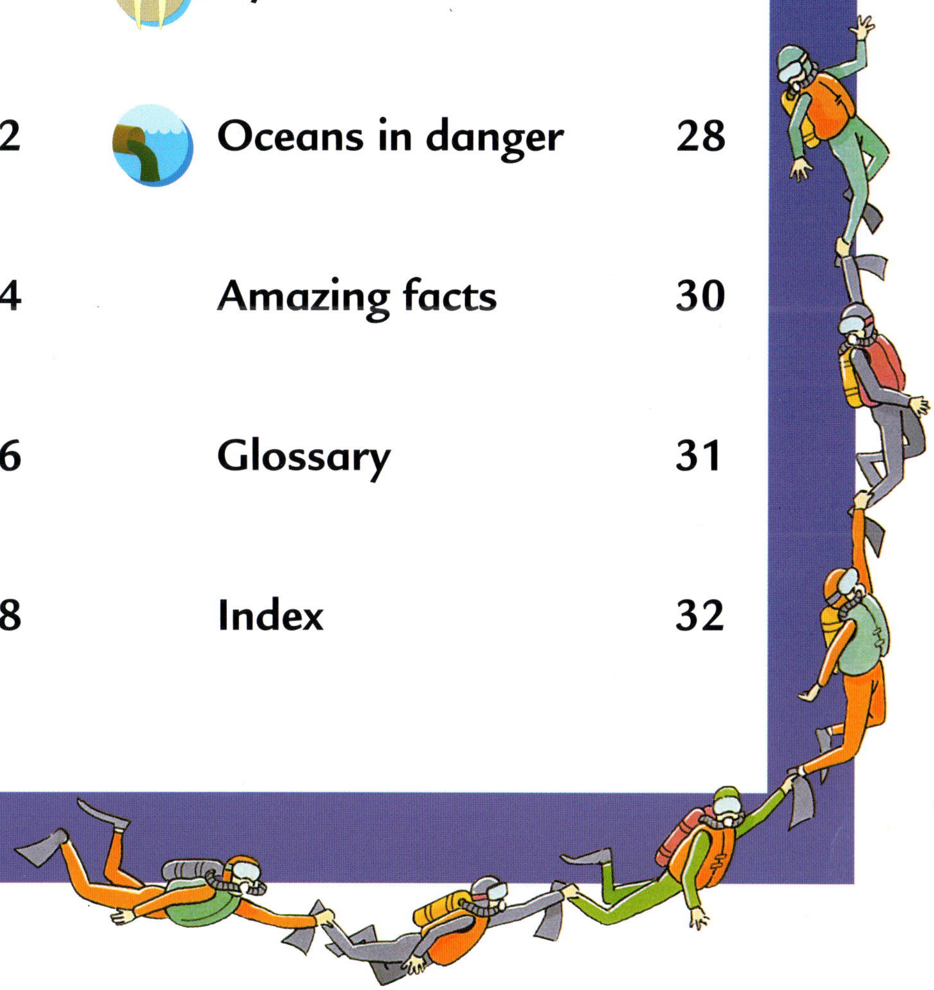

Oceans of the world

Oceans cover over half of the Earth. Oceans are huge, but sometimes they are divided into smaller areas called seas. Some parts of oceans are deep, dark and cold, while others are shallow and warm.

The living oceans

Beneath the waves, oceans are full of extraordinary animals, from tiny fish to huge whales. Some of the most important animals are so tiny you cannot see them. They are called **plankton** and are food for larger animals.

Under the water

The bottom of the ocean, or seabed, does not always look the same. It can be muddy, sandy or rocky. Sometimes it is flat, but it can also have mountains or deep narrow ditches, called trenches.

▶ It is fun to play in the sea when it is calm.

◀ **In some warm, shallow waters, brightly coloured coral reefs grow. Many fish search for food or hide from enemies among the coral.**

Water on the move

Oceans are always moving. They are pulled by **currents** which carry water to different parts of the world. Currents are caused by winds, the spinning of the Earth and the **temperature** of the land.

Powerful waves

The wind blows the surface of the ocean into waves. On a calm day, the waves are small, but when there is a storm, the waves are bigger and the water becomes rough. When waves crash on to the **seashore**, they slowly wear away rocks on the **beach**.

Quiz Corner

- How much of the Earth is covered by oceans?
- Does the bottom of the ocean always look the same?
- What makes waves?

look at: Oceans of the world, page 4, Shallow waters, page 10

Seashore

Twice a day, the sea moves up the seashore, then falls back down again. These movements are called tides. At high tide, the sea has moved as far up the seashore as it can. At low tide, it has moved back down again. Tides mean that many animals that live on the seashore are used to being both wet and dry.

CHATTERBOX

The oceans of the world flow into one another, so things that fall into the ocean may end up thousands of kilometres from where they were dropped. Often, coconuts are found far away from the tropical islands where they grew.

An anemone catches food with stinging* tentacles. *If it is attacked, it can pull in its tentacles.

A scallop belongs to the same group of animals as the slug. Its shell comes in many shapes and sizes.

A lugworm lives in the cool damp sand. Other creatures, such as crabs, hide in the sand, waiting for the tide to come in.

A water snail attaches itself to a rock with its suckers. Its shell keeps it safe from enemies.

giant clam

Molluscs

The ocean is full of animals with soft bodies, called **molluscs**. These animals are an important food for other ocean creatures.

Most molluscs live in shells, which protect them. Some molluscs, such as mussels and oysters, have two shells, which are held tightly together. When molluscs feed, the shells open. This lets sea water pass over fine hairs that pick out tiny pieces of food. If the mollusc feels threatened, the shells close up quickly.

oysters

A sea urchin has a soft body protected by prickly spikes. It eats plants and tiny animals on the rocks.

A starfish has five arms which it uses to crawl over the seabed. If a starfish has an arm bitten off, it grows a new one.

A limpet has a cone-shaped shell. It grips the rocks so tightly, it is almost impossible to pull it off.

Quiz Corner

- How often does the sea move up and down the seashore?
- Why do molluscs live in shells?
- Where can seashore animals hide when the tide is out?
- Can a starfish grow a new arm?

look at: Seashore, page 6

The crab family

Crabs, lobsters, prawns and shrimps belong to a family of animals called crustaceans. They have soft bodies with a hard outer shell, called an exoskeleton. This shell protects them from hungry predators. Crustaceans eat any food they can find on the seabed and seashore.

How crabs grow

A crab cannot grow in the same way as many other animals because it has a hard shell outside its body. When the crab becomes too big for its shell, the shell cracks open to show a new shell inside. This hardens in a few days.

▲ A crab has eight legs for walking and two arms with big **pincers** for cutting up and eating food.

▼ A hermit crab does not have its own hard shell, so it lives in the shell another sea animal has left behind. As the hermit crab grows, it moves to a larger shell.

Lobsters

Usually, lobsters hide during the day and hunt for food at night. They have one pincer which is bigger than the other. They use their big pincer to crush **prey**, and the smaller one to cut it into bite-size pieces.

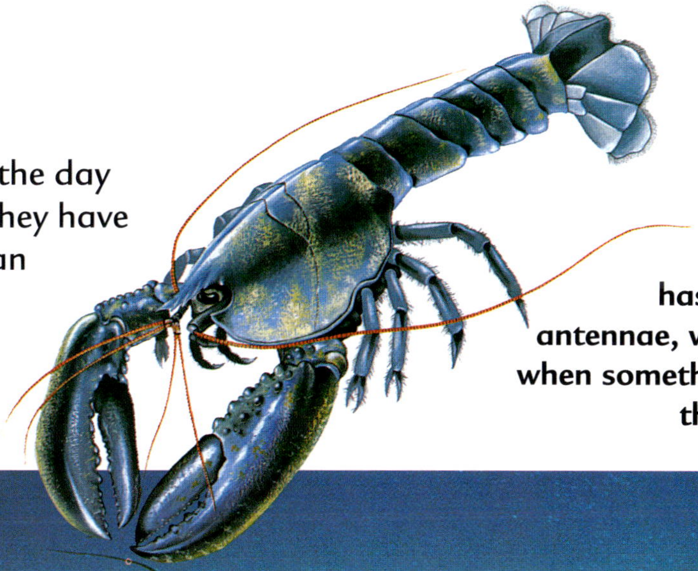

◀ A lobster has long feelers, or antennae, which let it know when something is moving in the water nearby.

▲ Every year, when storms hit Florida, in the United States, large groups of spiny lobsters walk in lines over the seabed to calmer waters.

A helpful shrimp

A cleaner shrimp eats tiny animals that crawl over fish. This helps to keep the fish clean. Although shrimps are a popular food for many fish, the helpful cleaner shrimp never gets eaten.

Quiz Corner

- How does the crab's hard outer shell help to keep it safe?
- What happens when crabs grow?
- How many legs do crabs have?
- Why do lobsters need feelers?
- Where does a hermit crab live?

look at: Seashore, page 6, Coral reefs, page 12

Shallow waters

The most shallow parts of the ocean, where the land slopes gradually into the water, are known as continental shelves. Here, sunlight reaches almost to the seabed, so plants, such as seaweeds and sea grasses, can grow. These waters are usually warm, clear and full of plankton.

▲ Seahorses live among seaweed. When resting, a seahorse holds on to the seaweed with its tail to stop it from floating away.

Plants without roots
Seaweeds belong to a group of plants called **algae**, which are different from plants that grow on land. Seaweeds do not have roots or flowers. Instead, they have holdfasts, which fix them to rocks or the seabed and stop them from floating away.

A small shark
Dogfish belong to the shark family. They lay their eggs among seaweed in a special case called a mermaid's purse. The purse has strings called tendrils to hold it on to the seaweed.

◀ Often, empty egg cases are washed up on the **seashore**.

▼ Kelps are the biggest seaweeds. Often, many kelp plants grow side by side. They form underwater forests which sway gently in the ocean water.

Quiz Corner

- What is a mermaid's purse?
- How are seaweeds different from other plants?
- What does a seahorse use its tail for?
- What are the biggest seaweeds called?

look at: Shallow waters, page 10

Coral reefs

In a few parts of the world, where the ocean is shallow, clear and warm, there are beautiful underwater gardens, called coral reefs. Reefs are made up of many types of coral, such as fans, horns, pipes or plates. Most corals are hard, but some are soft and sway in the ocean currents.

Different types of coral

Coral is formed from millions of tiny animals called coral polyps. Different coral polyps form different shapes.

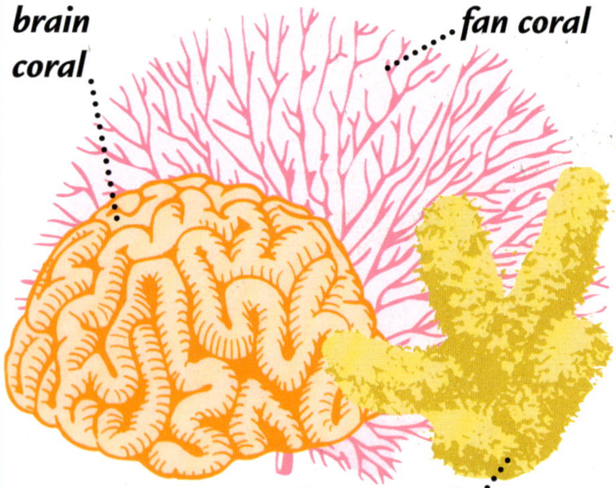

Hiding places

Coral reefs are full of hiding places, such as tunnels, caves and tiny holes. They make safe homes for many ocean creatures. Often, small fish can dodge between the corals to escape from bigger fish that are trying to eat them.

▲ The Red Sea in Egypt has a large coral reef. Scuba divers find many colourful fish there, such as this sabre squirrelfish.

Quiz Corner

- What tiny animals form coral?
- Where do you find coral reefs?
- Why do many sea animals live in coral reefs?
- Where can you find sabre squirrelfish?

look at: Shallow waters, page 10

The open ocean

The oceans of the world are home to thousands of different kinds of animals. These animals spend most of their time looking for food or trying not to be eaten. Many travel long distances in search of food. Others drift where the ocean currents take them.

How do fish breathe underwater?
Fish breathe underwater through special flaps called **gills**. A fish sucks water through its mouth and pumps it across its gills. This moves a special gas called **oxygen** from the water into its blood.

Life under the waves

Different types of ocean creatures live in different parts of the ocean. Some, such as flatfish, stay close to the seabed to hunt for food. Others, such as turtles, live near the surface of the water because they need air to breathe.

A sea snake has a flat tail that works in the same way as a paddle, helping it to wriggle through the water.

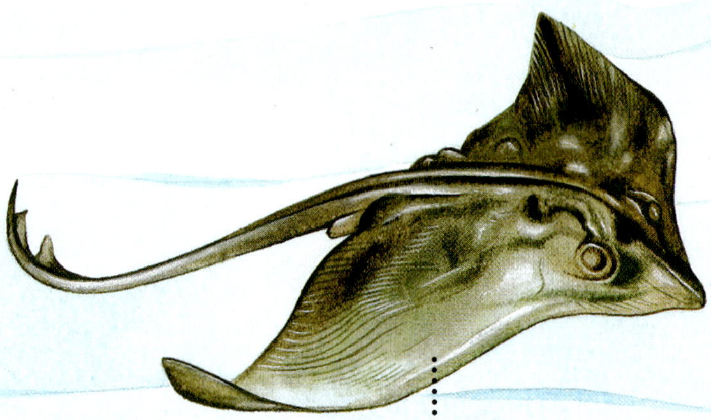

A plaice, like other flatfish, lives on the seabed. It has eyes on top of its head, so it can see what is happening above.

A ray has a flat body and fins that look similar to wings. It seems to fly through the water. An electric ray can give its ***prey*** *a powerful electric shock.*

Quiz Corner

- Which part of their bodies do fish use to breathe?
- Why do some fish travel in shoals?
- How does a jellyfish catch its prey?
- How does a sea snake swim?

◀ A group, or shoal, of fish swim together for safety.

A flying fish can leap out of the water and skim over the surface.

Swimming shoals

Some fish swim in huge groups, called shoals. A shoal can make it difficult for **predators** to pick out one fish to eat. Sometimes a shoal can even be mistaken for one enormous fish.

A turtle lives most its life in the ocean, travelling enormous distances across the warm waters of the world.

A jellyfish drifts through the ocean, waiting to catch prey in its long, stinging ***tentacles.***

look at: The open ocean, page 14

Creatures of the deep

Light cannot reach the bottom of the ocean, so deep down it is always cold and dark. Many deep-sea animals have clever ways of making their own kind of light to help them see. They are also good at catching food which is often difficult to find.

Glowing in the dark

Ocean animals that glow in the dark use light in many different ways. Some jellyfish flash to frighten enemies. Anglerfish use light to make their **prey** or a mate come towards them. Others, such as flashlight fish, use light to signal to each other, or to help them to see when they are hunting.

flashlight fish

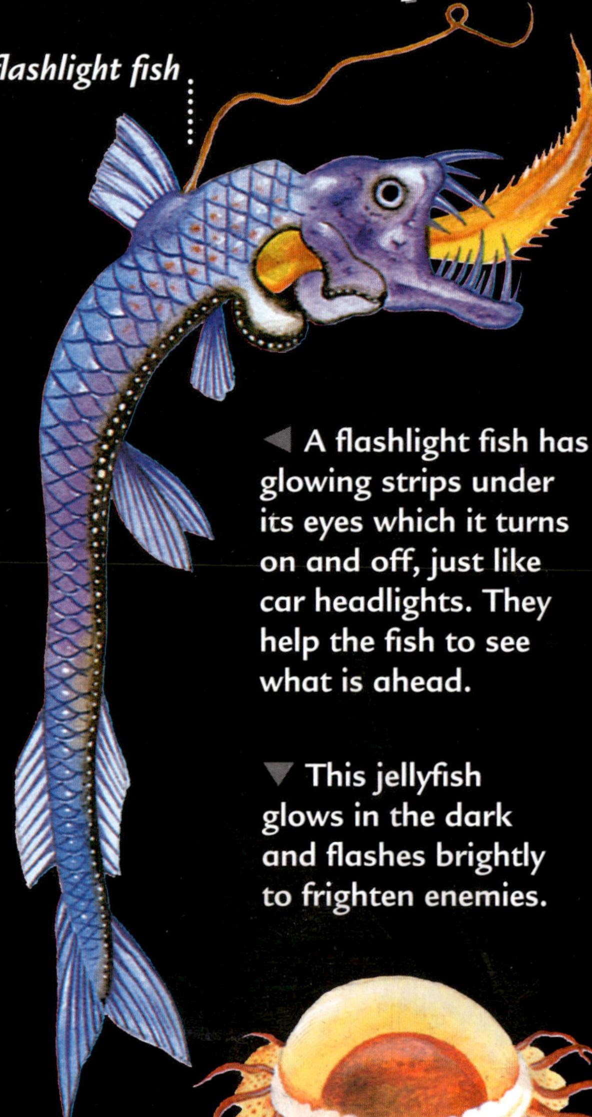

◀ **A flashlight fish has glowing strips under its eyes which it turns on and off, just like car headlights. They help the fish to see what is ahead.**

▼ **This jellyfish glows in the dark and flashes brightly to frighten enemies.**

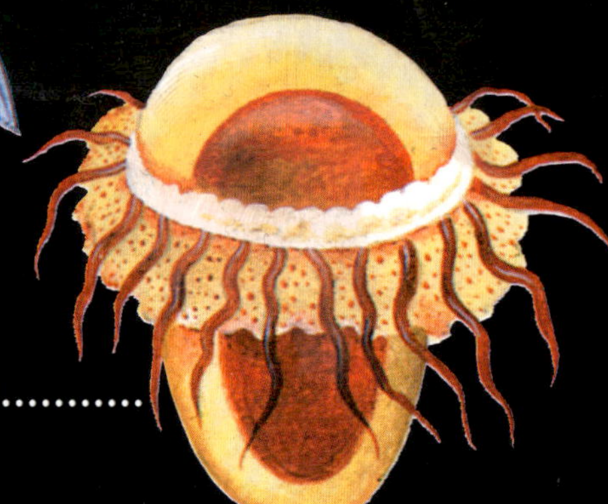

jellyfish

◀ **An anglerfish has a rod that grows from the top of its head. The rod glows to make other fish come towards it. In the dark, prey cannot see that they are swimming straight into the mouth of the anglerfish.**

CHATTERBOX

The swallower fish has a stretchy stomach which can hold a fish almost as big as itself. One meal can last the swallower fish a long time.

▲ Brittle stars, tripod fish and sea cucumbers live on the seabed in the deepest parts of the ocean. They eat any food that sinks to the bottom.

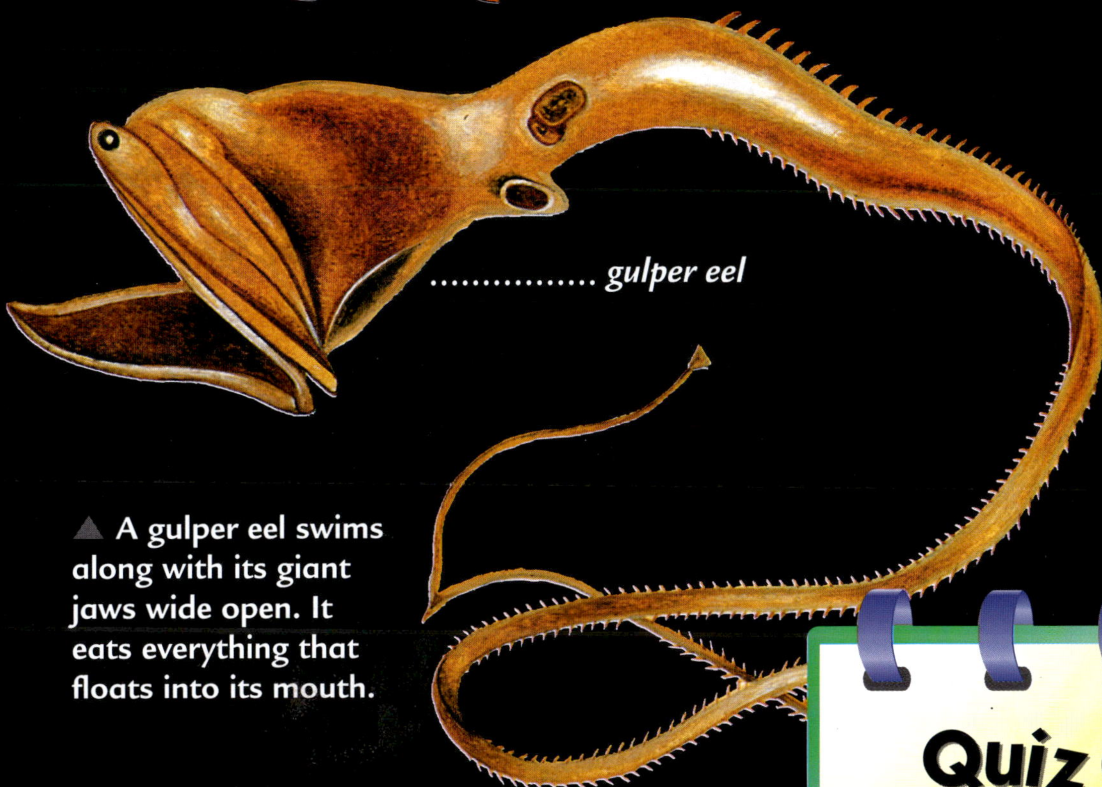

▲ A gulper eel swims along with its giant jaws wide open. It eats everything that floats into its mouth.

▲ Lantern fish are common deep-sea fish. On moonless nights, they rise to the surface of the water to eat **plankton.**

Quiz Corner

- Why is it always cold and dark deep down in the ocean?
- Why does a gulper eel swim with its jaws open?
- How does an anglerfish catch its prey?

look at: The crab family, page 8, The open ocean, page 14

Octopuses and squid

Octopuses and squid belong to a group of animals that have tentacles. An octopus has eight tentacles with suckers on the bottom. The tentacles help the octopus to move over the seabed. The suckers help it to grip its food or to hold fast when a predator is trying to attack.

Clever creatures

Many scientists believe that octopuses are clever creatures. They have discovered that octopuses learn quickly and can even do tasks, such as taking a cork out of a bottle. In experiments, octopuses have also been known to steal food from one another's tanks.

▼ A squid has eight short tentacles for swimming and two longer ones for catching food.

CHATTERBOX

A giant squid can be over 15m long – that's as long as seven divers swimming hand to flipper. There are even stories of these monsters wrestling with sperm whales.

SEE FOR YOURSELF

You can see how an octopus or squid swims by squirting out water from its body. Blow up a balloon, but not too much, then let it go underwater. As air escapes, the balloon whizzes off in the same way that an octopus or squid moves.

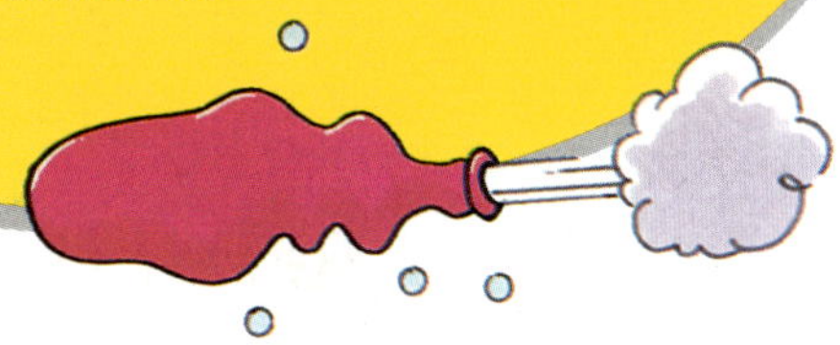

Keeping safe

Octopuses and squid can hide from enemies by changing their colour. This is called **camouflage**. They can also squirt out a cloud of special ink which makes it difficult for enemies to see them in the water.

▼ A giant octopus lives deep down in the ocean. It has eyes which are 17 times larger than a human eye.

Quiz Corner

- How does an octopus move?
- What does an octopus use its suckers for?
- When does a squid use its two longer tentacles?
- When would an octopus or squid squirt out a cloud of ink?

look at: The open ocean, page 14, Creatures of the deep, page 16

Sharks

Sharks are the world's biggest fish. Some sharks are great hunters with razor-sharp teeth, but others eat only tiny plankton. Sharks have excellent hearing and can pick up the sound of splashing water from far away. They also have a good sense of smell and can sniff out animals that are hurt and will be easy prey.

◀ A sand tiger shark has sharp, strong teeth for killing prey.

A full set of teeth
During a shark's lifetime, it has thousands of teeth which grow in rows. As soon as a tooth from the front row breaks or falls out, one from the row behind moves forward to take its place.

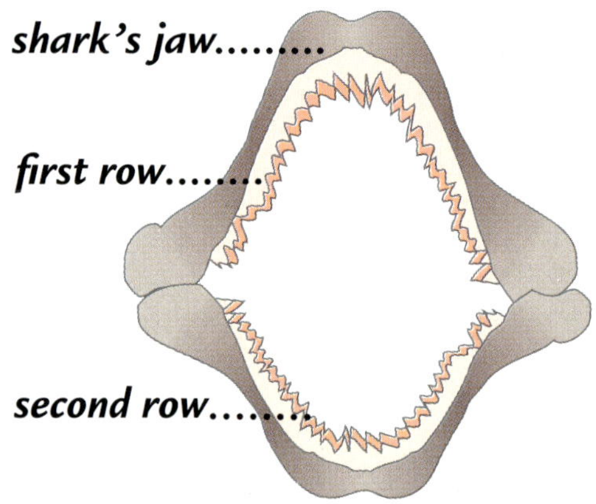

The great white shark
One of the most dangerous kinds of shark is the great white shark. It is a powerful hunter with strong jaws and enormous, jagged teeth. Usually, a great white shark eats animals, such as seals. Occasionally, it attacks people.

Strange heads

A hammerhead shark has a strange-shaped head with one eye and one nostril at each side. When the shark hunts for food, it swings its head from side to side, so that it can see all around its body. Some types of hammerhead shark are hunted by humans for their skin and oil.

CHATTERBOX

Sharks have to keep swimming all the time. If they stop, even for a little while, they sink.

▶ A hammerhead shark is a fast and powerful swimmer.

▼ When hunting prey, a great white shark can swim five times faster than a person. Its smooth, rounded body and strong tail help it to move quickly through the water.

Quiz Corner

- Why are sharks such good hunters?
- What happens if a shark's tooth falls out?
- Are great white sharks dangerous to people ?
- Why are hammerhead sharks hunted?

look at: The open ocean, page 14, Octopuses and squid, page 18

The whale family

The largest ocean creatures are whales. They belong to a group of animals called mammals. Dolphins and porpoises belong to the whale family. They are called toothed whales and have small, sharp teeth for eating fish and squid. Whales, like all other mammals, need air to breathe. They take in air through blowholes on the top of their heads.

Big and blue

The blue whale is the biggest whale of all and is probably the largest animal that has ever lived on Earth, including the biggest dinosaur. A fully grown blue whale is about the size of a large jumbo jet. It is also the noisiest animal in the world. It moans and grunts loudly to other blue whales.

Baleen whales

There are two types of whales, baleen whales and toothed whales. Baleen whales do not have teeth. Instead, they have a row of furry plates, called baleens, that look like a comb. Baleen whales eat only tiny sea animals, called krill, that can pass between the plates.

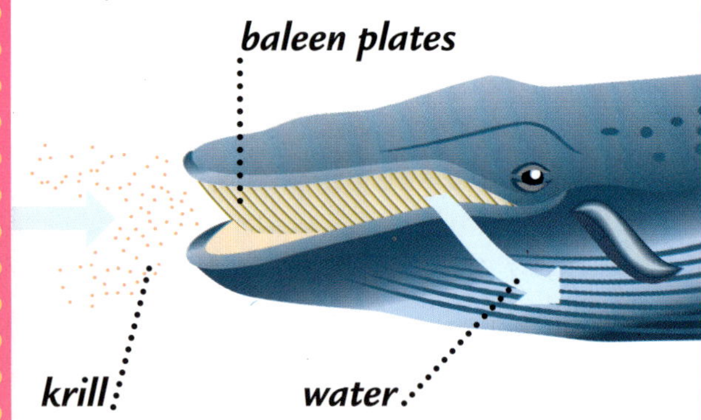

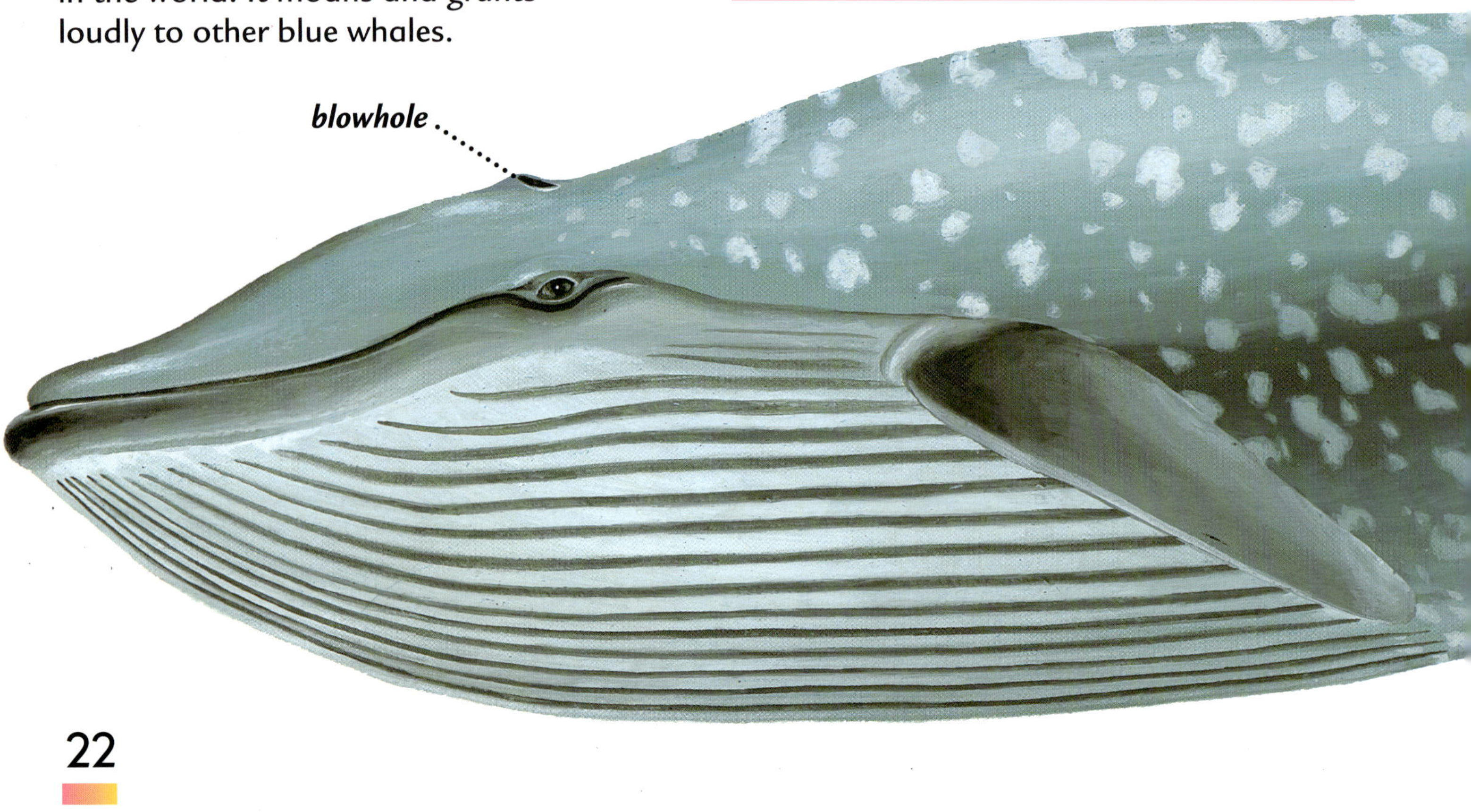

Dolphin or porpoise?
Dolphins and porpoises look alike, but there are ways to tell them apart. Dolphins have long, beak-shaped snouts and rounded teeth. Porpoises have rounder snouts and flatter teeth. Dolphins also live in large groups while porpoises usually prefer to live alone.

► **Bottlenose dolphins hunt for fish in a group. They also like to play together and often leap out of the water at the same time.**

▲ **The blue whale has an enormous appetite. A fully grown adult eats huge amounts of krill every day.**

Quiz Corner

- **How do whales, dolphins and porpoises breathe?**
- **What does a baleen whale eat?**
- **What is the shape of a dolphin's snout?**
- **Which is the biggest whale of all?**

look at: Seashore, page 6, The open ocean, page 14

Sea birds

Some sea birds live on the seashore. They have long legs for wading in shallow water and thin beaks for picking out food from mud or sand. Other sea birds live far out at sea. They are good at flying and spend weeks in the air. When they come back to land, they find it hard to stand up. All sea birds return to the seashore to lay eggs.

◀ Many sea birds spot fish from the sky, then dive after them at great speed.

▼ Gannets, like many other sea birds, live in large groups on steep rocks and cliffs.

SEE FOR YOURSELF

Many gulls lay their eggs on narrow cliff ledges. The eggs do not fall off the cliffs because they are a special pointed shape. If they are knocked, they just roll in a circle. You can test this by making your own pointed eggs out of Plasticine and watching how they roll.

Long-distance flyers

An albatross is a large sea bird with long, strong wings. It can fly over the oceans for months at a time. When an albatross flies, it hardly flaps its wings. It simply glides through the air, carried by the wind.

▲The black-browed albatross visits land only to lay eggs and look after its chicks.

Quiz Corner

- Why do all sea birds return to the seashore?
- How do many sea birds catch fish?
- Which sea bird can fly over the ocean for many months at a time?

look at: The whale family, page 22

Icy waters

Around the North and South Poles, parts of the ocean are frozen, but they are still full of life. Animals that live in and around these frozen oceans, such as fish, seals and whales, are used to living in the cold. Seals have thick layers of fat, called blubber, to keep them warm and some fish have special blood which does not freeze.

CHATTERBOX

No one has ever found a mermaid, but there are many stories about this strange creature that is half-fish and half-woman. Most people now believe that mermaids are really walruses.

▲ Walruses usually live together in large groups. They use their two long front teeth, or tusks, to dig for food on the ocean floor. Walruses also use their tusks to fight off polar bears.

Seals and sea lions

Seals and sea lions look similar to each other, but you can tell them apart. Sea lions walk around on dry land using their strong front flippers, while most seals have weak front flippers and just slide around on their stomachs.

▼ **Adélie penguins look clumsy on land but they are good swimmers. They stay in the sea for weeks at a time.**

▲ **A seal dives deep down into the water looking for fish to eat. It cannot breathe underwater, so closes its nose until it comes back to the surface.**

Penguins

A penguin is a bird that cannot fly. On land it waddles on its short legs, but underwater it swims as fast as a seal. It uses its wings as flippers to move through the water quickly and its webbed feet to turn. As it swims, the penguin's white stomach makes it difficult for **predators** to spot it from below.

Quiz Corner

- What is blubber?
- What does a walrus use its tusks for?
- Why do penguins have white stomachs?
- How can you tell the difference between a seal and a sea lion?

look at: Seashore, page 6

Oceans in danger

All over the world, people eat animals from the ocean. But nowadays we are catching too many fish and there may not be enough left for the future. Oceans are also becoming polluted. We must take care of our oceans to keep them safe for us and the animals that live in them.

▲ Even large animals, such as this fur seal, can become caught in rubbish. An animal may push its head through holes in a net, then find it cannot free itself.

Don't leave litter

Do not throw rubbish into the sea or leave it on a **beach**. If you do, the rubbish will sit on the seabed or be washed up on another beach. This rubbish can harm animals, who may become caught in it or try to eat it. Always take your rubbish home and put it in a bin.

▲ In some countries, waste from factories is dumped straight into the sea. This can kill animals living there.

CHATTERBOX

One salmon farmer has a clever way of keeping seals away from his fish. He uses a model of a killer whale to scare them off!

Too many fish?
Fishermen have become so good at catching fish that many countries now have strict rules about how many fish they can catch. Fishermen are not allowed to use nets with small holes because these nets catch too many fish. If nets have big holes, young fish can escape and **breed**.

Quiz Corner

- **Why do some fishermen use nets with small holes?**
- **Why is it wrong to throw rubbish into the sea?**
- **Why should we protect the oceans?**
- **Can fishing nets hurt large animals?**

▼ Small fishing boats catch fewer fish than large ships. This means more fish are left in the oceans to breed.

Amazing facts

● Dolphins have their very own language. They talk to each other by making chirping and clicking sounds.

☆ *Mother penguins can find their own chicks on a crowded iceberg. To the mother's ears, each baby chick sounds different and she can pick out her own chick just by listening for its cry.*

● Did you know that whales can sing? Underwater, their songs can be heard for hundreds of kilometres. The grunting song of the blue whale is louder than the engine of a jet plane!

☆ *The world's smallest fish is the dwarf pygmy goby, which lives in the Pacific Ocean. It is about the size of a baked bean!*

● Male seahorses are good fathers. Their job is to look after the female's eggs. They carry them around in a special pouch hidden underneath their bodies until the eggs are ready to hatch.

☆ *A giant blue clam is a type of mollusc that can live for over 100 years. Sometimes it makes a precious stone, called a pearl, in its shell.*

● Sea snakes kill fish with a poisonous bite. Just one drop of their strong poison is enough to kill three people.

☆ *A starfish has a strange way of eating. It can push its whole stomach out of its body and on to its unlucky prey. The prey stays covered by the starfish's stomach until it has been completely eaten.*

● Hermit crabs can grow to many different sizes. Some are as big as your hand, but others are as small as a pea.

☆ *A female sea turtle lays her eggs on a sandy seashore. She leaves the baby turtles to hatch without any help, but they know exactly what to do. As soon as they hatch, they quickly run down to the sea.*

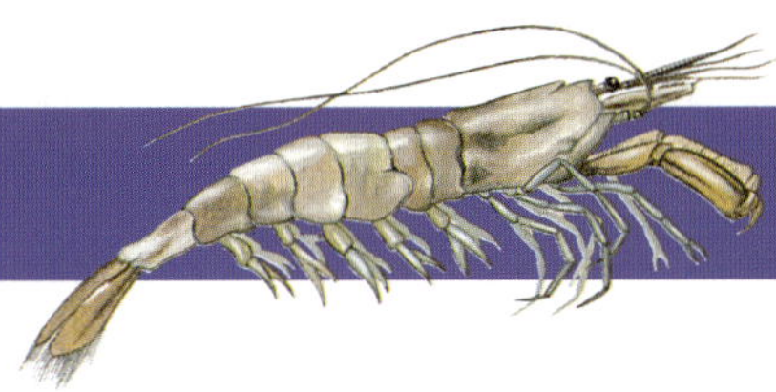

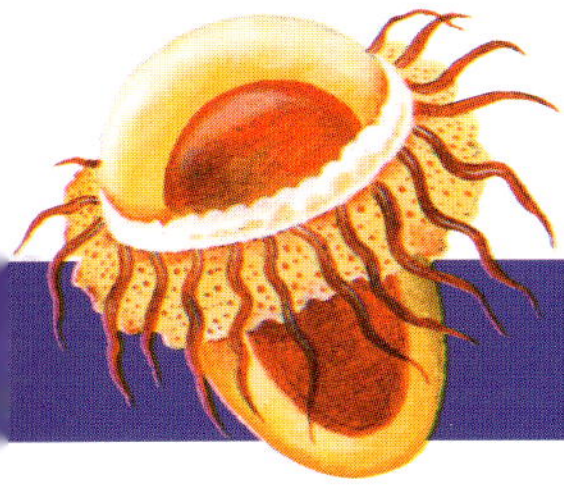

Glossary

algae The family of plants to which seaweeds belong.

beach A stretch of land by the ocean's edge, usually covered by sand or small pebbles.

breed When any creature makes young of its own kind.

camouflage A disguise that hides something, usually so that it looks like its surroundings. This confuses enemies.

continental shelf The shallow part of the seabed just off the **seashore**.

crustacean A creature that has no bones. A hard outer shell called an exoskeleton covers its body.

current A large amount of water or air that flows in one direction.

gills A part of the body that absorbs **oxygen** from water. Animals with gills can breathe underwater.

molluscs Animals with soft bodies that do not have a backbone. Some molluscs live in a hard shell to protect their soft bodies.

oxygen A gas that is found in air and water. All plants and animals need oxygen to live.

pincer A very strong claw made up of two parts that close tightly to hold or cut things.

plankton Very tiny plants and animals that live in the sea.

polluted Something that has been damaged by other substances.

predator An animal that hunts other animals for food.

prey An animal that is hunted by another animal for food.

seashore The land by the edge of the ocean. Often, water moves on to this land.

temperature How hot or cold something is.

tentacles Long feelers, rather like arms, that can be used to catch or hold things.

tides The rise and fall of the sea level at the ocean's edge.

Index

Published by Two-Can Publishing,
43-45 Dorset Street, London W1U 7NA

For information on Two-Can books and multimedia, call (0)20 7224 2440, fax (0)20 7224 7005, or visit our website at http://www.two-canpublishing.com

Text: Francesca Baines
Consultant: Matthew Robertson
Watercolour artwork: Stuart Trotter
Computer artwork: D Oliver
Commissioned photography: Steve Gorton
Photo research: Dipika Palmer-Jenkins
Editorial Director: Jane Wilsher
Art Director: Carole Orbell
Production Director: Lorraine Estelle
Project Manager: Eljay Yildirim
Editor: Deborah Kespert
Assistant Editors: Julia Hillyard, Claire Yude
Co-edition Editor: Leila Peerun

'Two-Can' is a trademark of Two-Can Publishing. Two-Can Publishing is a division of Zenith Entertainment Ltd, 43-45 Dorset Street, London W1U 7NA

Hardback ISBN 1-85434-963-5
Paperback ISBN 1-85434-969-4

Dewey Decimal Classification 910

Hardback 2 4 6 8 10 9 7 5 3 1
Paperback 2 4 6 8 10 9 7 5 3 1

A catalogue record for this book is available from the British Library.

Printed in Spain by Graficromo S.A.

Photographic credits: Bruce Coleman (C&S Hood) p12-13, (Hans Reinhard) p25r; Oxford Scientific Films (Fred Bavendem) p18t, (Max Gibbs) p10t, (Howard Hall) p9c, (Richard Hermann) p11, (William Patton) p24-25; Photographers Library p4-5; Planet Earth Pictures (Peter David) p16b, (Ken Lucas) p21c, (William Smithey) p28t, (Norbert Wu) p8b; Tony Stone Images p5t, p20t, p26, p29; Telegraph Colour Library FC, p23t; Zefa p15t, p19, p27, p28b.

Title previously published under the Launch Pad Library series